TRUMPED

ST. MARTIN'S GRIFFIN

NEW YORK

A John Boswell Associates Book

TRUMPED

THINK LIKE A BAZILLIONAIRE

by

Donald J. Trumped

AS TOLD TO JOHN BOSWELL

www.stmartins.com

BOOK DESIGN BY AMANDA DEWEY

ISBN 0-312-34085-0

EAN 978-0312-34085-8

First Edition: October 2004

10 9 8 7 6 5 4 3 2 1

Dedication

I would like to dedicate this book to the people most important to ME. Without them I would not be where I am today. You know who you are, but just so you get to see your names in print: Cindy Adams, Larry King, Jay Leno, Liz Smith, Oprah Winfrey, Regis Philbin, Matt Lauer, Katie Couric, Robin Leach, "Page Six," the Money Honey, *Dateline NBC*, the *Access Holly-wood* crew, and the gang over at *ET*.

And this is for you,
Arthur Ochs Sulzberger Jr.

About This Typeface

This book is set in special 14-point type, Trumped Type™, which I own. I like this typeface because it's **big** and **bold** and just a little bit **fat**. Like me.

Okay. Let's get the bad joke out of the way: Any reproduction or use of this typeface without my express written consent and, well, you're fired.

How to Use This Book

- Carry this book in your breast pocket. If you are ever shot in the heart by someone with excellent aim who is using a very weak gun, this book will save your life.

- Place this book on top of your head and walk around with it. Try not to let it fall off. This is how to develop poise.

- Place this book on someone else's head next to a wall, so that the book is actually touching the wall. Now draw a short line under the book. The distance between the line you have drawn and the floor is the person's *exact* height.

Dare to Be Me

*Great quotations look even
greater when set in italics.*
—DONALD TRUMPED

Y ou are not going to be-
lieve this book. In my opinion, it is the greatest
book ever written. Actually, I haven't read
every book ever written. So let's just say it's the
greatest book written in the last thousand years.

Some have speculated that because my time is so valuable I have used ghostwriters to write all my previous books. Yes, I have. Then again I personally polish the prose into dazzling gold— not just any gold of course, but twenty-four karat gold, which I own, imported from India on the backs of elephants. Not just any elephants but elephants that actually swam here with the gold on their backs!

You will soon get to see these elephants perform at the fabulous Trumped Taj Mahal Hotel and Casino in Atlantic City, New Jersey, which I own. In my opinion, it is the finest gambling venue in the world. First class all the way. Yes, it *is* on the verge of bankruptcy, but *my* money is safe. While I am indeed the majority shareholder, I have absolutely nothing to do with running the place.

Forbes magazine has again picked me as one of the richest individuals in the world. They estimate my worth to be $2.4 billion. Now don't get me wrong. *Forbes* magazine is a great magazine. It is one of the finest business magazines in the world, but their estimate is way, way low. Other than to say it's around a bazillion dollars, I don't want to get into specifics. Let me put it another way. If I were offered $2.4 billion dollars for all of my assets, would I take it? The answer is no. And neither would any of the banks that own them.

My motivation in writing this book is to show you how to think like me, how to act like me, even how to eat like me. Does that mean that by reading it you will become obscenely rich, ridiculously famous, and a world-class babe magnet? Of course not, but by the time you get this far, you will have already paid your ten bucks, so I'm doing just fine. In fact, you have already learned Lesson #1: Never judge a book by its cover.

A Minute in
the Life

In all of my previous
books, or at least some of them (I better go back
and make sure I've read them all), I've included
a chapter that describes—in diary form—a typi-
cal week in my life. Since I've received so much
positive feedback, and since it's a great way to
fill up empty pages, I'd like to do it again. Only

this time, to provide a little more texture and give a better sense of how fast-paced my life really is, I've limited the time frame to one minute:

9:00:01 Admire new $18,000 Rolex Oyster Rockefeller wristwatch bought from street peddler for $20 after bargaining him down from $50. *Nobody* outnegotiates the Donald.

9:00:03 Call Frank's Deli, make offer on large coffee, glazed donut. Five bucks, take it or leave it, and no charge for immediate delivery.

9:00:04 Offer accepted. Do I know this town or what?

9:00:06 Look at the newspapers: *New York Times, Post, Daily News, Wall Street Journal.* No mentions of me on front page, no pix. Toss out papers.

9:00:08 Notice itch on back of neck.

9:00:09 Scratch itch.

9:00:11 Itch gone. See a problem—solve a problem. Definition of a *doer!*

9:00:14 Midlife crisis. Is this how I want to spend the rest of my life?

9:00:15 You bet it is!

9:00:16 End of midlife crisis.

9:00:17 Make prank call to Tiffany's. Remind them I own the air rights for their building. *So stop breathing so much!* Ha, ha, ha, ha!

$

9:00:28 Tap wristwatch sharply with forefinger.

$

9:00:29 Hold watch up to ear. *No ticking sound.*

$

9:00:32 Check classy solid-gold-covered chocolate desk clock for time.

$

9:00:33 Look out window. Greatest view in the world! Street peddler still there at corner of Fifty-seventh and Fifth. (Greatest address in the universe!)

9:00:34 Call Jimmy "Mother" Cabrini, head of Consumer Relations. Ask him to interview street peddler for possible position on *The Apprentice*. Simple qualification test: Can he hold his breath underwater for two hours?

$

9:00:44 Sneeze.

$

9:00:46 God bless me!

$

9:00:47 Thank me very much.

$

9:00:50 Something in left nostril.

$

9:00:51 Got it! As always, I pick a winner!

$

9:00:52 Turn on TV to Spanish-language Telebimbo channel.

$

9:00:53 Ooogle babes doing Sambaerobics on beach at Ipanema.

$

9:00:55 Make note: In tropical-theme drinks served at fabulous Trumped Copacabanana Casino, next to little umbrella, put in tiny beach chair, itsy-bitsy towel.

$

9:00:57 Review layout of new Trumped Multinational Golf Course. Approve concept of longest hole in world, 955 yard par-7 and toughest hole in world, 176 yard par-2.

$

9:01:00 End of another terrific New York minute!

The Trumped Magic

Other than "Spare change?" the question I get asked the most is How do you do it? How do you take these rundown buildings in marginal neighborhoods and turn them into the finest residential and commercial properties in the world?

Well, I've been doing this for quite a while,

and in the parlance of my industry I am what is known as "a real professional." In other words, this is what I do professionally.

Over the years I have developed a hard-and-fast set of rules for turning dilapidated old buildings that are about to fall down into sleek new condos that are about to fall down. These rules are what you might call *The Seven Habits of One Highly Effective Real Estate Developer*, or what you could call *The Seven Pillars of Trumped Wisdom*.

1. If it's still standing, sheath it in reflective glass.

2. Spend your money where it counts the most—on the elevator interiors.

3. Use only the finest Dominican silks and Puerto Rican marble.

4. There's nothing that can't be improved with gold-plating.

5. Carpets don't need to be thick, but they should be tall.

6. The giant chandelier, made of thousands of individual little pieces of glass, should make a crinkly sound when the wind blows.

7. When in doubt, slap a mirror on it.

7A. Hire high-ranking uniformed Uzbekistanian military officers to stand outside your buildings.

The Best Financial Advice I Ever Received

Several years ago I had occasion to visit in person with my Swiss banker, Dieter Von Bertelsmann. I was blindfolded and taken to an undisclosed location. The Bertelsmann's ties to the banking business go back for several generations, but they are so secretive, no one knows for sure how many. After World War II, Dieter's grandfather, Jingleheimer Bertelsmann, smuggled hundreds of millions of dollars of stolen art out of Germany. Unfortunately for Dieter, he refused to tell anyone where he hid it. This is a family that knows how to keep a secret.

I told Dieter that I had been highly dissatisfied with my financial advisors—that under their guidance my return on capital was barely more than I was paying to borrow it. "Dieter," I said, "is there some safe, surefire way to double my money every year?" I will never forget the words that came out of his mouth.

"Herr Donald," he said, "*Du spartest, dächt' ich, solche Sprüche; Hier wittert's nach der Hexenküche, Nach einer längst vergangnen Zeit. Mußt' ich nicht mit der Welt verkehren? Das Leere*

lernen, Leeres lehren? Sprach ich vernünftig,
wie ich's angeschaut, Erklang der widerspruch
gedoppelt laut; Mußt'ich sogar vor widerwärti-
gen Streichen Zur Einsamkeit, zur Wildernis en-
tweichen Und, um nicht ganz versäumt, allein zu
leben, Mich doch zuletzt dem Teufel übergeben.
Ich bin ein Amerikaner."

The 10 Commandments of Business

1. **Get your retaliation in early.**
2. **There is no job so big or so small that there won't be plenty of other people to blame.**
3. **Speak loudly and carry a big stick. Well obviously you need to speak loudly so people can hear you, and once you get used to walking around with a big stick,**

you will be amazed at how many uses you will find for it.

4. Eliminate the middleman—and make sure he doesn't float back up to the surface.

5. If you can't think of something nice to say, that's why they invented e-mail.

6. Accentuate the positive, eliminate the negative, and don't mess with Mr. Inbetween.

7. When the going gets tough, take the bull by the horns and run with it.

8. Hmmm. What else? Okay, here we go: Never whittle toward yourself.

9. Wow. This is really hard. I'm running on empty here. All right, how about this one? Never stick anything in your ear smaller than your elbow.

10. Never *ever* commit to doing a list of ten of anything until you know what all ten are.

The Bazillionaire Diet

Let's face it. There are only so many sides of Kobe beef and boxcars of Beluga caviar that you can eat in one lifetime. (By the way, the one-lifetime-per-human thing is really starting to bother me. I need to figure that one out—and quick.)

Also, the health police were starting to get to me. Seemed that the better food tasted and the more expensive it was, the worse it was for you. So two years ago I decided to completely change my diet. From that moment on I decided to eat only money.

Now don't get me wrong. I don't eat *just* money. Sometimes I'll grab a junk bond for a quick snack or a penny stock for a pick-me-up. When I really want to reward myself, I might have a fancy meal of debentures and arbitrage worksheets.

I do miss the old days when I would travel to Europe and have a truly international meal of francs, lira, marks—maybe a few kroners for dessert. Honestly, once you've tasted one Euro, you've tasted them all.

I'll eat a little yen now and then, though they

can be a little fishy tasting. I've completely sworn off the Chinese yuan. An hour later and I'm hungry again. Also, when I ask the waiters, "Do you have 'flied lice'?" they never seem to get it.

Why I'm Not Running for President

T

Y ou may recall that in 2000 I seriously considered running for president of the United States. I seriously considered it again this year, and have once again decided against it. Quite frankly, it feels pretty good to consciously decide every four years that I'm *not* running for president. Anyway, here are my reasons:

$

1. Hard to believe, but the finances of the good old U.S.A. are even shakier than mine.

2. Could never live in the White House. Not my style. Too much old stuff.

3. Thanks to Mister Banana Pants Clinton, no babes in the Casa Blanca.

4. Three branches of government, two too many.

5. Wouldn't get as much media coverage as I do now.

6. Where the heck is Iowa?

7. *Air Force One:* No hot tub or sexy flight attendants.

8. U.S. presidents don't get to wear cool uniforms.

9. Can't build up in D.C. (height restrictions). Can't even buy air rights.

10. Have to visit places where there are poor people.

Get A Pre-Shackuptial

T

I've said it over and over again (in fact, I had the nerve to repeat it in all of my books): Always get a pre-nuptial. If I hadn't had a pre-nup, Ivana would have absolutely taken me to the cleaners. So get a pre-nup . . . and never marry a Czechoslovakian.

I believe the pre-nup is such a great concept,

I now apply it to all aspects of my social life. Before I have a cup of coffee with some lovely lady, I first have her sign a pre-cuptial. Dinner? A pre-suptial. Breakfast? A pre-sunnysideuptial.

Before calling her on the phone, I have my lawyer deliver a pre-calluptial. In case I have to cut the call short, it includes a codicil—the pre-hanguptial.

And, of course, always, *always*, get a pre-shackuptial.

The First
Rule of
Advancement

The first rule of advancement is this: In any hierarchical organization, know when to kiss ass and when to kick ass. If it's above you, kiss it; if it's below you, kick it; and if it's on the same level, screw it.

Here is a simple technique for remembering

which is which: You kiss with your mouth (above);
you kick with your foot (below).

Follow this one rule and I'll be seeing you
soon at YPO meetings.

Creative One-Upsmanship

T

The problem with most very rich people is that not only are they greedy, they are totally lacking in creativity when it comes to showing off. They all buy the same things—paintings they'll never look at, exotic cars they'll never drive, mansions they'll never set foot in. (Having said that, I do want to begrudgingly express my admiration of Tyco's Dennis Kozlowski. Creating an ice sculpture of Michelangelo's Statue of David and then coming up with the idea of having real champagne shoot out his penis—that's inspired.)

I try to spend my money more creatively. I mean, when everyone else has two Rolls, three Bentleys, and a warehouse full of custom Ferraris, where's the envy in that?

When I play golf, for instance, I bring along an entire female entourage—fourteen caddies, one for each club; Arianna, whose only job it is to wash my balls; and Trixie, my designated ball marker. My favorite moment is on the green when Trixie marks my ball, then hands the ball to Arianna, who washes my ball before handing it to me. That's what I call making them "green with envy." (Ha! Ha!)

Another project I'm working on—though I don't plan on finishing it anytime too soon!—is that I've set aside some land in Manhattan's old West Side train yard, which I own, for the Trumped Tomb. It's going to be this ziggurat kind of thing completely covered in—you guessed it!—reflective glass.

Also, for next to nothing—I mean they positively gave it to me—I bought the mountain from the National Park Service next to Mount Rushmore. You've seen pictures of it in the background a thousand times, but for obvious reasons you've never noticed it before.

Now called Mount Trumpmore, and soon to feature the very large image of yours truly, it will overlook my new theme park, Trumpland.

Okay, so Michael Jackson had the idea before I did, but did he have The Apprentice Coaster—up, down, up, down, up, down, just like the fortunes of my contestants?—I think not.

The Art
of the
Small Talk

T

Because everything I say is big and important, I feel challenged when it's time to make small talk.

One of my most embarrassing moments came one day when I was having lunch with Henry Kravis and Ron Perelman. I told them that even though I took a *short*cut on the way over, I still found myself feeling *short* of breath. I asked Hank if he'd been thinking about selling a particular stock *short*. I asked Ron if he was feeling *short*changed by Revlon's Board-of-Directors. My God, I couldn't stop saying the word "short." I even recommended they order the *short* ribs! Boy, was my face red.

Anyway, I meet thousands of new people every day and everyone of them expects me to say something brilliant or profound. So I've developed a list of short pithy comments—"small talk," if you will—that meets everyone's extremely high expectations of me.

Feel free to use them yourself—I haven't trademarked them yet—and once I do, I'll be collecting.

And, as that old saying goes "Have a nice day!" ☺

$

1. "Hot enough for you?"

2. "Much traffic on the way over?"

3. "How 'bout them Cowboys?"

4. "Oooo-whee! The price of gasoline!"

5. "Do you think these glasses make me look smart?"

6. "How much do you think I paid for this watch?"

7. "Pass the Grey Poupon."

Talk to
The Hair

I've taken a lot of flak lately about my hair. Most of the criticism has been good-natured, but some of it has been downright nasty. (Don't think I'm not taking names.)

So I want to let you in on a little secret about my hair. My hair is much more to me than just my hair. It is my constant companion, my advisor, my confidant, my best friend.

My hair actually speaks to me. (For some reason, it has a very high voice, like Mickey Mouse.) It also has magical powers and can accurately predict the future. When I asked The Hair if I should do *The Apprentice*, it responded, "Outlook good." When I asked if I should marry Marla, it said, "Reply hazy, try again." Get into beauty contests? "Signs point to yes." I once ignored my hair, to my own peril. Years ago I asked about my future in casino gambling. "Don't count on it," The Hair said.

My hair also has certain hypnotic properties. When I mesmerize people, they often think it's my beady little eyes. It's not. It's The Hair.

How *The Apprentice* Came To Be

Tast year I was approached by Mark Burnett who, singlehandedly, invented reality TV. Mark created *Survivor*. He is a first-class producer and a world-class human being.

He had read my books and said that not only

had they changed his life but that, in his opinion, after the Bible, they were the greatest books ever written.

I said, "Who'd a thunk it?"

He laughed heartily. In fact, he laughed so heartily he couldn't catch his breath. Tears were coming from his eyes and snot was running out his nose.

I was starting to warm to this man.

He explained his *Apprentice* concept to me and described the role of mogul/mentor he wanted me to play. "Why me?" I asked.

"Mr. Trumped," he said, "because you are quite simply the greatest human being who ever lived. You have it all: looks, brains, smarts, hair, taste, style, panache, pizzazz, presence, charm, chutzpah, halvah, zip, pow, shazam, flash, savvy, you name it. You are boss, rad, phat, bad, groovy, and hip. A great humanitarian, a noble citizen, a fine parent, a sage counselor, a caring ex-husband, a force for good, a true genius, and a loyal friend."

I liked his style.

The rest, of course, is television history.

Think Inside
the Box

"**T**hink outside the box." "Think outside the box." Ugh! (I'm putting my finger down my throat.) If I hear that phrase one more time I think I'm going to throw up.

And whenever I think I'm going to throw up, that's a good time to look for opportunity. So here's what I came up with: Think *inside* the box.

That's right. Think inside the box. Makes sense, doesn't it? With everyone else thinking outside the box, there's plenty of space inside the box to come up with dull, boring, unoriginal business solutions.

Let me give you an example of how I make inside-the-box thinking work for me. There's this large parcel of land in Westchester County, which I own, and upon which I planned to build the world's greatest golf course—but the planning commission wouldn't let me. Something about using too much water, as though water were some kind of precious natural resource. This was obviously very shortsighted on their part. Now the residents all have to drive cross-county to Briarcliff Manor to play the greatest golf course in the world, which I also own.

So I'm thinking to myself, "What's the inside-the-box solution? What's the most dull, boring use I can make of this land?" Then it hit me: *Put up a bunch of houses*. And that's exactly what I'm doing.

Of course, these won't just be any houses. These will be Trumped Houses. Mansions, really. Actually, more like estates. Trumped Estates. Which I will own.

How I
Always Get
My Way

T

Many people are amazed by how often I seem to get my way. I do, in fact, get my way just about all the time, but it's hardly by accident. It takes patience, a singleness of purpose, and a willingness to stay the course. But most of all—and I think I'm go-

ing to surprise a few people here—it takes . . .
niceness.

That's right. I think that being nice is the
most important element in getting people to see
things your way.

Here's a perfect illustration of "niceness in
action" that took place several years ago. That
idiot governor of ours was trying to encourage
New York State Indian tribes to build gambling
casinos on their tribal land.

As you can imagine, this would not have been
in the best interests of my Atlantic City opera-
tions. Fortunately, this was something that had
to pass through the state legislature, and several
of the most influential legislators happened to be
good friends of mine. Sensing that these legislators, who should probably remain nameless,
could use a little R&R, I arranged to have the
Trumped jet fly up to Albany to pick them up

and take them down to Mar-a-Largo, my world-class resort in Palm Beach, Florida. There they were each met by two highly intelligent young women who saw to their every need for the duration of their stay.

I'm not saying that my kindness in this particular instance influenced their vote, but it has been five years now and how many ground breakings for Indian casinos in New York State have you heard of?

I had a similar experience when I was building my Westside Condos in Manhattan. I had passed all the necessary ordinances and received all the required permits and the only thing that was preventing me from getting started was one of these annoying little local neighborhood associations that fiercely opposed just about everything I planned to do.

Obviously, the head of this association was,

by definition, a loser. So I thought to myself, "What would make a loser like him feel like a winner like me?" The answer occurred to me right away: I sent over a brand new set of matching Louis Vuitton luggage each filled to the brim with large denominations of used, unmarked U.S. currency. Let me say, I was not surprised when this local neighborhood association immediately withdrew all its objections.

Always Wear
the Same Suit

T

I am a great believer in both quality and quantity. Indeed, one of my goals is to own one of everything.

Take my wardrobe. Look at any photo taken of me over the last thirty years and you will see that I am always wearing the same blue suit.

It is the finest suit ever made, handcrafted by

Brioni in Italy then shipped to Switzerland where every thread was reinforced with titanium. This is why it has lasted so long and why it never looks rumpled.

Why do I choose to wear this one suit when I could afford to own thousands of them? First, I know exactly what I'm going to look like every day even before I get dressed. (For a long time I also only owned one tie—a red one. In recent years, however, I've expanded my wardrobe to four ties: a red one, a pink one, a blue one, and this kind of shiny powder-blue thing.)

Second, I have to make thousands of decisions each day and I'm not going to waste one of them on something as silly as what suit to wear.

Finally, because my suit is titanium-reinforced I never have to send it to the cleaners. Just a little steel wool gets rid of even the most pesky stains.

How to Become A Bazillionaire

T

1. Inherit $100 million.
2. Borrow $900 million from the bank.
3. Buy a bunch of buildings and beauty contests.
4. Tell everyone that you're a bazillionaire. (What? Are they going to ask to see your bank statements?)

Scare the Shit Out of Them

Remember Trumped Television City? That was the property I was developing on the West Side of Manhattan. It was to be the site of the world's tallest building, the most renowned television production facilities anywhere, and eight thousand of the finest residential units in the universe.

I'll let you in on a little secret. Television City was bullshit from the get-go.

All I ever intended to build were a bunch of shoe-box condos that would overtax facilities and overpopulate the area. I knew this would never get past the various planning boards and neighborhood watchdogs. I knew this because every single person who has ever lived on the West Side of Manhattan is a Big Loser.

So I proposed this outrageous monstrosity that would have never been approved in a million years. When I "scaled back" to just a bunch of cheesy condos, everyone was so relieved I barely needed to fill out the paperwork.

Right now I'm preparing a bid to buy Central Park. Do I expect it to succeed? Of course not. But don't be surprised when you see the new Trumped Fancy Spa Resort & Marina going up where the zoo used to be.

Brand
Everything

T

The Trumped brand, which I obviously own, is the most valuable real estate brand in the world. I will continue to grow the brand both vertically (Trumped Slums) and horizontally with: convenience stores (Trump-Mart); miniature golf courses (Trump Putt); and gentlemen's clubs ($trumpets).

Why is branding so important? First, it adds value. Second, as I think I have proven time and again, it adds value for absolutely no valid reason whatsoever.

It has been reported that I am trademarking the phrase, "You're fired," which I invented. This is true, and I will soon be introducing the You're Fired brand of charcoal lighter fluid.

In fact, I intend to brand pretty much everything. By this time next year, I should own picnics, Sweet Sixteen, "Dude," and "Hasta La Vista, Baby."

Another reason to brand is to discourage competition. For instance, down the road, I plan to trademark the vowels: a, e, i, o, u, and possibly y. Vowels are used throughout the world except in countries like Croatia and Slovenia. While I obviously will not be able to cash in every time someone uses a vowel, neither will anyone else.

Win-Wynn

T

"Win-win." That's another one of those trite, overused business expressions that every time I hear it makes me want to gag. (I'm pretending to stick my finger down my throat.)

According to Negotiating 101, win-win means that both sides get something out of a deal and both sides walk away feeling good about themselves. That way, a bond of trust is formed—a relationship—and the two parties will want to work with each other again.

In my experience, that never happens. The next time around the guy's been fired or he died or the company's gone bankrupt or the more you get to know 'em the more you get to hate 'em.

I believe in living in the present—get all you can today and let tomorrow take care of itself. I also believe, however, in win-Wynn, named in honor of Steve Wynn, who, to this day, thinks he's one of my best friends.

You've heard of Steve Wynn. He's a Vegas guy. Built the Bellagio. Sold it. Owned this big art collection. Sold that too.

Anyway, back in the mid-seventies, when I bought this Atlantic City property from the Paris Hilton Hotel chain, Steve Wynn had the nerve to bid against me. Well today, that property is called the Trumped Marina, not the Wynn Marina or the Trumped & Wynn Marina. I didn't have much choice but to stomp all over the guy.

That's where "win-Wynn" comes in. Win-Wynn states that in any negotiation, it's not how much the other side gets out of the deal that counts; it's how much you can make the other side *think* they got out of the deal that counts.

In this particular case, I convinced Steve that it was no great shame to get pounded by someone like me. In fact, quite the opposite. Just going up against someone like me showed that he had real *cojones*. That should be worth a lot to him.

To this day, whenever I run into Steve, he thanks me for the time I kicked his butt and for all the great publicity he was able to get out of it.

"No problem," I say (wink, wink). "Always happy to help out."

Take Your
Ego to Lunch

T

With all the phenom-
enal success I've had, sometimes there's a dan-
ger of starting to believe my own press notices,
particularly those that quote me directly. So just
to keep my head screwed on straight, I make it a
point to take my Ego out to lunch on a regular
basis. Although I have a monster Ego, it is easily

gratified and doesn't need to eat much for Ego fulfillment.

Occasionally my Id insists on tagging along. I try to discourage it because, frankly, my Id is obnoxious, always looking past me for something better—and female—to come along. And when it zones in on an attractive young lady? It lets go with this lecherous "heh, heh, heh" Bevis-type laugh. Way creepola.

I once tried to take my Ego on an ego trip, but it was a total disaster—too much baggage. When we do get some time alone, what do we talk about? Me, mostly, but my Ego doesn't mind because I always pick up the check.

TRUMPED

The Best Sex She Ever Had

When my second marriage fell apart we managed to keep most of the details out of the press. In the hopes of helping those of you whose own relationships may be a little rocky, I want to share a couple of the not-great things that went on between us.

The biggest problem was that Marla had these ridiculous fantasies that I was supposed to be some kind of real person or something. One evening I came home absolutely exhausted from a long day of building monuments to myself, and Marla said to me, "The toilet in the Roman bath is stuffed up. Can you unclog it?"

I looked at her like she was out of her mind. "What?" I said. "Do I *look* like a plumber?"

About a week later I walked in and she said, "All the lights are out in the Liberace Music Room. Can you put in a new fuse?" I just stared at her in disbelief. "What?" I said. "Do I *look* like an electrician?" What planet was this woman living on, anyway?

Then there was that other thing.

I went out of town for a week, I came back home, and everything worked. All ninety toilets were flushing. All the lights were brightly burning. Someone even fixed that little plug in the rear of the coffeemaker and set all the clocks back to Daylight Savings Time.

"Who'd you get to fix all this stuff?" I asked.

"You see that cute guy getting on the elevator when you came in? He did everything."

"Great," I said. "How much did it set us back?"

"Nothing," she said. "He told me that if I were to either bake him a cake or go to bed with him, he wouldn't charge me a cent."

"So you baked him a cake?"

Marla looked at me like I was out of my mind.

"WHAT?" she hissed. *"Do I look like fucking Betty Crocker?"*

Do You Have What It Takes to Be *The Apprentice*?

T

The response to the first season of *The Apprentice* has been so phenomenal that for the new shows, we received 70 million applications! In order to go through so many, we had to devise certain loaded questions, meaning that if you didn't get the right answers, you were automatically rejected. I thought it might be useful to share some of these questions with you, although certainly not the answers because we might use some of them again (heh! heh!).

1) My associate on the show, Caroline:

    a) has a spoke up her ass

    b) is a real hottie

    c) could use a good spanking

    d) all of the above

2) Are you of some exotic ethnic background or blonde?

3) Reading comprehension:

    "No Man is an island."

3i) According to this passage, no man is

    a) an isthmus

    b) a peninsula

c) a lagoon

d) an island

3ii) A good title for this passage would be:

a) *Meet Mr. Muskrat*

b) *The Amazing Spleen*

c) *Baku: Pearl of the Caspian*

d) *Man Is Not An Island*

4) Finance: Two frillion kajillion godzillion dollars minus two frillion kajillion godzillion dollars =

a) $0

b) $1 frillion

c) $2 kajillion

d) $2.2 godzillion

5) Are you, or have you ever been, related to Mark Burnett and what's the story with this guy? Did he have a real life before Reality TV?

6) Which of the following represents the best new business opportunity:
- a) opening a real estate 'n' cheese shoppe
- b) selling mink-lined hot tubs
- c) drive-thru dentistry
- d) nail salons for pets

7) Have you ever worked with anyone of Italian descent in the concrete or waste management industries?

8) What do you think of my hair?

9) Would you be willing to eat live centipedes? Oops, wrong show (ha! ha!).

10) Would you be willing to:
- a) dress up like Diana Ross
- b) dance with a pole
- c) show your tits
- d) get a good spanking

Golf, Like War, Is Hell

T

Being the Big Winner that I am, it probably comes as no great surprise to you that winning at the game of golf is just as important to me as winning at the game of business or winning at the game of love or winning at the game of life or winning at the game of

Yatzee. Whether I'm playing a million-dollar Nassau or for something *really* significant, I want to beat my opponent. If I can thoroughly humiliate him in the process, then all the better.

I would love to shoot a great score every time I go out, but even *I* can have a bad day. Strategically, therefore, I see competitive golf as a battle that is waged on two fronts: Not only are you trying to take strokes off your score, you are also doing everything in your power to help your opponent add strokes to his score.

The point to remember is this: There is nothing more fragile than a golfer's psyche. If you can get inside your opponent's head and create a little self-doubt, he might as well pay up the money he owes you now.

I have a whole bag full of psychological tricks I can pull out for almost any golfing situation.

Naturally, I don't want to give away all of them, but here are a few just to give you some ideas:

$

- Always take a mulligan on the first tee, no matter how good your drive, then play the better of the two shots. Your opponent will become so unhinged he may not even call you on it, but even if he does, your utter disregard for the Rules of Golf will play with his head for at least the next several holes.

- Similarly, always improve your lie on the first fairway, or rough-onto-fairway, as the case may be. I generally try to make a show of it—getting down on one knee and pinching together the grass to make a little "pillow" for the ball.

- If there is water on the left or a dogleg right say, "Wow, look at this hole! Good thing you always play a fade." If there is water on the right or a dogleg left say, "Wow, look at this hole! Good thing you always play a draw."

- If he hits a great drive when you're on the next tee say "Wow, that last drive must have traveled close to three hundred yards" or "Show me what you did with your grip to get that extra power."

- If he's on a hot streak say, "Wow, what's that? Three pars in a row?" or "Wow, par in from here and you'll break 80."

- If he misses a short putt, pump your first in the air and shout, "You the choker!"

- If he's stupid enough to ask you for your advice about anything, tell him he's not swinging hard enough.

"I Believe . . ."

Every great executive should have a strong core-belief system. In fact, one of my core beliefs is that every great executive should have a strong core-belief system. There are many other things that I believe in as well. Here are just some of them:

I believe that my word is my junk bond.

I believe that when you walk a mile in another man's shoes, you should get to keep them.

I believe it's not whether you win or lose, but how you rig the game.

I believe that a fool and his money represent a great opportunity.

I believe that you should not borrow money from anyone named Vinnie.

I believe that you should not accept wooden nickels, tin dimes, or $100 bills with my picture on them.

I believe that Bud Light has great taste *and* is less filling.

How
I Handle
Criticism

For someone like myself, who pretty much spends every waking moment in the public eye, it is not surprising that I may occasionally rub someone the wrong way. Throw in my monster success and the capacity for some people to be insanely jealous, and the criticism

I've occasionally received may even be somewhat unfair.

When I think about my critics, if I think
about them at all, which I actually do quite a bit,
rather than respond impulsively, I have trained
myself, first, to consider the source of the criticism. As it turns out, almost all my critics tend
to fall into one of three categories: First, Is this
guy an asshole, or what? Second, Is this guy a
major asshole, or what? Or third, Is this guy the
world's biggest asshole, or what?

Once I've considered the source, I'm a great
believer in "Don't get mad, get even." I also believe that, whenever possible, the punishment
should fit the crime, although those opportuni-
ties rarely present themselves. I do remember
one time when I was relandscaping Mar-a-Largo,
this guy delivered eight tons of fertilizer when
I'd only ordered four, and then refused to take

any of it back. So I filled this paper bag with dog poo, put it on his front porch, set it on fire, then rang his doorbell and ran away. I think he knew who did it, but he couldn't let on just in case it wasn't me.

I remember another time when Graydon Carter, who is now editor of *Vanity Fair* but was then at *Spy* magazine, referred to me in print as a "short-fingered vulgarian." So I called Domino's and had them deliver two hundred pepperoni pizzas to *Spy*'s offices (I think there were only ten people working there!)

Whenever someone was rude to me on the phone, I used to have all these great phone pranks I could play on them, but, unfortunately, caller ID has pretty much put me out of the phone-prank business. What I will still do occasionally is have my secretary call up maybe ten times and say, "Can I speak with Don?" Then I'll call up and say, "This is Don. Any messages for me?"

For me, personal confrontations are the most difficult because I don't really have time to "consider the source" and automatically jump to putting the offender into my third category. One time I was at this prestigious charitable function, and this other real estate developer, whom I've always considered a major loser anyway, got right in my face and shouted, "You're a big, fat, obnoxious blowhard!"

The whole room came to a complete stand-still, waiting to see how I was going to respond. I have absolutely no idea why this came to me but it did and, very coolly, I replied, "I'm rubber. You're glue. Bounces off me and sticks to you." I turned and walked away.

You could have heard a pin drop.

The Power of Positive Delusion

I'll be the first to admit it. I am a great believer in the extreme power of extremely positive thinking. I'm not so much a cockeyed optimist as I am a blind-as-a-bat optimist. For me, not only is the glass not half empty, it's never even half full. It's filled to the brim, running onto my table, dripping onto the floor and staining my very nice, expensive carpet.

To anyone who might say to me, "Donald, haven't you taken this power-of-positive-thinking thing to the point of detachment, that your unbridled optimism has only a passing acquaintance with reality?" I would say to them, "What's so great about reality? Reality is having to make good on bond payments. Reality is sitting around watching yourself get old. I'll take delusion, thank you."

What I hope I have shown you in this book is not just how to be really great, but how to *fool yourself* into believing that you actually are as great as you pretend you are. Someone once said to me, "Donald, anyone who thinks they are as great as you think you are must be covering up for something. Like maybe a poor self-image or low self-esteem."

That's why I felt I needed to write this book—almost out of a sense of duty. Because when you take away all the pomposity and grandiosity, when you peel away all those layers we use to conceal our real selves from others, what you get with me at the core is the greatest self-esteem of any person who ever lived in the entire history of the world.

What's Next for Me

I know what you're probably thinking. "Donald, with your success, with your uncanny knack for turning total crap into pure gold, what could you possibly do to top yourself?"

My answer would be, "Dance with the super-model that brung you." In other words, more of the same, only bigger, better, and more mind-numbing.

I'll be writing more books of course—a lot more. Obviously I don't need the money but I still have many important things to say that people need to hear. To accommodate my prolific output, I'll soon be launching the Trumped Tome-of the-Month Club with the first three selections being *One-Minute Mogul*, *If You Swim with the Sharks Bop Them in the Nose*, and *Who Ate My Cheese-Its?*

I have a number of reality shows in development, many of them somewhat derivative of *The Apprentice*, including *The Asskisser*, *The Gossip Monger*, *The Backstabber*, *The Buckpasser*, and *The Clockwatcher*. I'm also developing a show for PBS, *Colonial Casino*, and for one of the networks, *Who Wants to Marry a Hooters Girl?*

I'm also buying up more beauty pageants as

fast as those little beauties can shake their booties. I need to be a little circumspect about my plans here, but just to give you one example, I have recently sewn up world rights to "Miss Brussel Sprout" that I will be moving from Davenport, Iowa to—get this—Brussels, Belgium!

Oh, yeah. I'll soon be announcing my plans to build the world's tallest building, but that's not really new since I make that announcement about every other year anyway.

Index

About the Co-Author

John Boswell is a New York book packager, business consultant, and author or co-author of sixteen books, including the classic business bestseller *What They Don't Teach You at Harvard Business School.* His other humor books include the *New York Times* bestselling *The First Family Paperdoll and Cut-Out Book, O.J.'s Legal Pad, Where's Saddam?, Bill Clinton's Little Black Book,* and *The Complete Book of Rationalizations.* His newest is *The Dysfunctional Family Christmas Songbook,* to be published Christmas 2004.